# "Rhythms of the Future: The History of Techno Music"

David Jack Gregg
www.tremendousprints.com

# CONTENTS

## Chapter 1: Origins of Sound: From Detroit to Berlin

The origins of techno music can be traced back to the streets of Detroit, Michigan, a city known for its rich musical heritage and vibrant cultural scene. In the early 1980s, a group of visionary artists emerged from this urban landscape, pioneering a genre that would revolutionize the electronic music landscape and captivate listeners around the world.

At the heart of this movement were three individuals who would become known as the Belleville Three: Juan Atkins, Derrick May, and Kevin Saunderson. These young artists, inspired by the futuristic sounds of electronic pioneers like Kraftwerk and the innovative spirit of their hometown, embarked on a musical journey that would shape the course of techno history.

Juan Atkins, often referred to as the "Godfather of Techno," drew inspiration from the soulful grooves of funk and the mechanical rhythms of German electronic music. He, along with Richard Davis and Jon-5, formed the group Cybotron and released tracks like "Alleys of Your Mind" and "Cosmic Cars," which showcased their unique blend of funk-infused electronic beats.

Derrick May, influenced by the eclectic sounds of European synth-pop and the emerging electro scene, started experimenting with drum machines and synthesizers. Together with Juan Atkins, he co-produced tracks under the moniker Rhythm Is Rhythm, crafting intricate compositions like "Strings of Life" and "Nude Photo" that pushed the boundaries of electronic music and became instant classics.

Meanwhile, Kevin Saunderson, heavily influenced by the energetic rhythms of disco and the soulful melodies of Motown, infused his productions with a distinct musicality that resonated with listeners. With tracks like "Big Fun" and "Good Life" released under the name Inner City, Saunderson brought techno to the forefront of popular culture, blending infectious grooves with uplifting lyrics.

These three artists, each with their unique styles and influences, came together to form the foundation of techno. They shared a common vision of creating music that reflected the industrial landscape of their city while embracing the possibilities of electronic instrumentation. Their early productions, often characterized by driving beats, synthesized melodies, and futuristic soundscapes, laid the groundwork for the genre.

But the story of techno goes beyond the music itself. It is also deeply intertwined with the cultural and social fabric of Detroit. The city, facing economic decline and social challenges, provided a fertile ground for artistic expression and experimentation. Abandoned warehouses and underground clubs became the playgrounds where techno thrived, offering an escape from the harsh realities of urban life.

As the sound of techno began to spread, it found a receptive audience in Europe, particularly in the city of Berlin. Berlin, a city divided by the Cold War, was undergoing its own transformation. The fall of the Berlin Wall in 1989 marked a new era of freedom and unity, and techno music became the soundtrack of this cultural revolution. The city's underground clubs and abandoned buildings became the breeding grounds for a burgeoning techno scene, drawing artists and enthusiasts from all corners of the globe.

The impact of Detroit's techno movement in Berlin cannot be overstated. The exchange of ideas and musical influences between these two cities created a symbiotic relationship that propelled the genre to new heights. Detroit artists like Juan Atkins and Derrick May performed in Berlin, sharing their music and expertise, while Berlin-based DJs and producers embraced the Detroit sound, incorporating it into their own creations. The cross-pollination of these two scenes gave birth to a unique blend of techno that reflected the spirit of both cities.

In this chapter, we have scratched the surface of the history of techno music, exploring its origins in the streets of Detroit and its expansion to the city of Berlin. The journey of techno is one of creativity, innovation, and cultural exchange, and it continues to evolve and shape the musical landscape to this day. As we delve deeper into the chapters that follow, we will uncover the pivotal moments, key players, and global impact of this influential genre. So join us as we dive into the rhythms of the future and unravel the captivating story of techno music.

## Chapter 2: The Birth of Techno: The Belleville Three

In the small suburban town of Belleville, just outside of Detroit, Michigan, a musical revolution was quietly taking shape. It was here, in the early 1980s, that three young friends and aspiring musicians—Juan Atkins, Derrick May, and Kevin Saunderson—would come together and lay the groundwork for what would soon be known as techno music.

The Belleville Three, as they would later be called, shared a common passion for electronic music and a desire to explore new sonic territories. They were influenced by a diverse range of musical styles, from the futuristic sounds of Kraftwerk to the soulful rhythms of Motown, and they were eager to carve out their own unique sound.

Juan Atkins, with his deep fascination for science fiction and a love for synthesizers, was the driving force behind the group's early experiments. Drawing inspiration from the mechanized beats of German electronic music, he sought to create music that captured the spirit of the times—a sound that was both futuristic and rooted in the urban landscape of Detroit.

Derrick May, known for his keen ear and ability to curate compelling DJ sets, brought a different perspective to the table. He was heavily influenced by the eclectic sounds of European synth-pop and the emerging electro scene, and he saw the potential for electronic music to transcend traditional genres and captivate audiences in new and exciting ways.

Kevin Saunderson, with his background in funk and disco, added a touch of musicality to the group's early productions. His understanding of groove and melody brought a soulful element to their tracks, infusing them with a warmth and depth that resonated with listeners.

Together, the Belleville Three began experimenting with drum machines, synthesizers, and early sequencers, pushing the boundaries of what was possible with electronic instruments. They were not content with simply imitating the sounds of their influences—they sought to create something fresh and innovative, a sound that was uniquely their own.

Their first foray into the world of music production came with the formation of their own record label, Metroplex Records. This independent label provided them with the freedom to release their music on their own terms, without the constraints of major record labels. It was through Metroplex Records that the Belleville Three released their early tracks, laying the foundation for what would become the sound of techno.

One of their most notable releases was Juan Atkins' "Alleys of Your Mind" under the moniker Model 500. The track, with its pulsating bassline and otherworldly synthesizers, encapsulated the essence of techno—a fusion of man and machine, of soulful melodies and mechanical rhythms. It quickly gained recognition in underground circles and set the stage for what was to come.

As their reputation grew, the Belleville Three began to DJ at local clubs and parties, spreading the sound of techno to an ever-growing audience. Their DJ sets became legendary, seamlessly blending tracks from different genres and eras into a cohesive and hypnotic journey. They were true pioneers, introducing electronic music to a city and a world that was hungry for something new.

The birth of techno was not a singular event, but rather a gradual process of experimentation, collaboration, and artistic exploration. The Belleville Three, with their distinct backgrounds and musical sensibilities, brought together the elements that would define the genre. Their fusion of futuristic sounds, infectious rhythms, and a deep-rooted connection to the Motor City gave birth to a musical revolution that would reverberate around the globe.

In the next chapters, we will explore how the Belleville Three's innovative sound caught the attention of the underground scene, leading to the rise of techno in Detroit and its subsequent spread across the world. We will delve into the underground movement, the emergence of influential techno pioneers, and the pivotal moments that propelled the genre into the mainstream consciousness. Join us as we continue our journey through the rhythmic landscape of techno music.

## Chapter 3: Underground Movement: The Warehouse Scene

In the early 1980s, as the sound of techno music began to take shape in the city of Detroit, a vibrant underground movement was brewing. It was a scene born out of a desire for musical freedom, where like-minded individuals gathered in unconventional spaces to experience the pulsating beats and hypnotic rhythms that defined techno.

One of the key catalysts for this underground movement was the rise of warehouse parties. These abandoned industrial spaces, with their raw and gritty atmosphere, provided the perfect backdrop for the immersive techno experience. Away from the constraints of traditional venues, these parties allowed DJs and producers to push boundaries and experiment with new sounds, creating a sense of liberation and exploration for both artists and attendees.

The warehouse scene became a sanctuary for those seeking an escape from the mainstream. It attracted a diverse and eclectic crowd, united by their shared love for techno and their desire to be part of something alternative and cutting-edge. These parties were not about glitz and glamour; they were about the music and the collective energy that filled the space.

The underground nature of these gatherings added to their allure. Word of mouth and flyers were the primary means of communication, spreading the details of upcoming events to a select few who were "in the know." The secrecy and exclusivity created a sense of anticipation and excitement, as attendees eagerly awaited the next warehouse gathering.

Inside these cavernous spaces, the music took center stage. The DJ, armed with crates of vinyl records and a deep knowledge of the genre, was the master of ceremonies, guiding the crowd through a sonic journey. The mixing of tracks, the seamless transitions, and the ability to read the energy of the dancefloor became an art form in itself, as DJs skillfully crafted sets that kept the crowd moving and entranced.

The warehouse scene also fostered a sense of community and camaraderie. Attendees formed connections and friendships, bonded by their shared passion for techno. It was a space where people could express themselves freely, where judgment was left at the door, and where the music served as a unifying force. The sense of unity and belonging was palpable, creating a unique and transformative experience for all involved.

But the warehouse scene was not without its challenges. As the popularity of these underground parties grew, so did concerns around safety and legality. The nature of occupying abandoned buildings posed risks, both in terms of structural integrity and potential legal repercussions. However, it was precisely this element of risk and rebellion that added to the allure and excitement of the warehouse scene. Attendees embraced the underground nature of these events, knowing that they were part of something unconventional and thrilling.

The impact of the warehouse scene extended far beyond the physical space. It served as a breeding ground for emerging talent, providing a platform for DJs, producers, and artists to showcase their skills and creativity. It nurtured a spirit of innovation and experimentation, where new sounds and styles were constantly being explored and refined. The warehouse parties became a testing ground for tracks and ideas, with the immediate feedback from the crowd influencing the direction of the music.

The influence of the warehouse scene on the development of techno cannot be overstated. It was here that the genre found its true home, free from the constraints of traditional venues and commercial interests. The underground movement fueled the growth of techno, attracting a dedicated following and creating a thriving subculture.

In the next chapters, we will explore the rise of key techno pioneers, the impact of techno in the global music landscape, and the fusion of techno with other genres. Join us as we continue our journey through the history of techno music and uncover the untold stories of its evolution.

## Chapter 4: The Techno Pioneers: Juan Atkins and Derrick May

In the early days of techno's development, two names emerged as the driving forces behind the genre: Juan Atkins and Derrick May. These visionary artists not only shaped the sound of techno but also laid the foundation for its cultural and artistic significance.

Juan Atkins, often referred to as the "Godfather of Techno," played a pivotal role in the genre's birth and evolution. Drawing inspiration from a variety of musical styles, including funk, soul, and European electronic music, Atkins was a true innovator. Through his solo projects and collaborations, he introduced groundbreaking tracks that merged futuristic sounds with infectious rhythms, creating a unique sonic landscape that would define techno.

Atkins's group Cybotron, formed in the early 1980s, produced tracks that set the stage for techno's emergence. Their seminal release "Clear" became an instant classic, blending robotic vocals, pulsating basslines, and intricate synth melodies. It was a futuristic vision of music, encapsulating the spirit of innovation and exploration that defined the genre.

Derrick May, another influential figure in the techno movement, brought his own distinct style and creative vision to the table. Known for his ability to craft mesmerizing DJ sets and his talent for production, May played a crucial role in popularizing techno both in Detroit and beyond. His tracks, such as "Strings of Life" and "The Dance," captured the essence of techno's emotive and soulful nature, bridging the gap between the underground scene and wider audiences.

Together, Atkins and May embraced the possibilities of electronic music, pushing boundaries and challenging conventions. Their collaboration on the track "Techno Music" further solidified their impact on the genre, with its hypnotic rhythms and futuristic soundscapes. They became pioneers of a movement that would transcend time and place, shaping the future of electronic music.

## Chapter 5: Detroit Techno Spreads its Wings: Inner City and Model 500

As techno music continued to evolve in the city of Detroit, new voices and sounds emerged, further expanding the genre's reach and influence. Among the prominent acts that emerged during this period were Inner City and Model 500, two projects that pushed the boundaries of techno and brought it to a wider audience.

Inner City, formed by producer Kevin Saunderson and vocalist Paris Grey, introduced a more accessible and commercially viable sound to techno. Their fusion of electronic beats with soulful vocals struck a chord with listeners worldwide, leading to chart-topping hits and international recognition. Tracks like "Big Fun" and "Good Life" became anthems of the techno movement, showcasing the genre's ability to captivate both underground and mainstream audiences.

Model 500, the brainchild of Juan Atkins, continued to push the boundaries of techno's sonic possibilities. Atkins, under the alias of Model 500, released a series of groundbreaking tracks that experimented with different styles and sounds. From the hypnotic grooves of "No UFO's" to the futuristic atmosphere of "Night Drive," Model 500 showcased the diversity and versatility of techno as a genre.

Both Inner City and Model 500 exemplified the growing influence of Detroit techno on the global stage. Their success demonstrated that techno was not limited to underground raves and niche audiences but had the potential to resonate with a wide range of listeners. These artists brought the spirit of techno to the masses, blurring the lines between genres and breaking down musical barriers.

In the next chapters, we will delve into the European takeover of techno, the impact of acid house on UK rave culture, and the crossover hits that propelled techno into the mainstream. Join us as we continue our exploration of the history of techno music and its profound impact on the musical landscape.

## Chapter 6: European Takeover: Techno Across the Continent

While techno music found its roots in the industrial landscapes of Detroit, it didn't take long for the genre to spread its wings and make its way across the Atlantic to Europe. The late 1980s and early 1990s saw a wave of techno's influence sweeping through the continent, with European artists embracing the genre and making it their own.

One of the key cities at the forefront of the European techno movement was Berlin, Germany. The divided city, which became synonymous with the Cold War, underwent a radical transformation following the fall of the Berlin Wall in 1989. The reunification of the city brought about a newfound sense of freedom and creativity, and techno music became a powerful expression of this social and cultural shift.

Berlin quickly became a hub for underground techno parties and gatherings. Abandoned buildings, warehouses, and open-air spaces became the playgrounds for ravers and techno enthusiasts. Legendary clubs like Tresor, E-Werk, and Berghain emerged as iconic institutions, hosting marathon techno sets and pushing the boundaries of electronic music.

The Berlin techno scene embraced a unique blend of dark, minimalistic, and industrial sounds. DJs and producers such as Paul van Dyk, Ellen Allien, and Sven Väth were at the forefront, shaping the sonic landscape of Berlin techno. The city's distinct atmosphere, coupled with its historical significance, provided a fertile ground for techno's evolution, allowing it to develop its own distinct character.

Beyond Berlin, techno found its way into the fabric of other European cities as well. In the UK, cities like London, Manchester, and Glasgow embraced the genre, spawning their own vibrant techno scenes. Acts like The Prodigy, Orbital, and The Chemical Brothers combined techno with elements of rave, breakbeat, and acid house, creating a unique British sound that resonated with a wide audience.

In France, the emergence of techno coincided with the rise of the underground rave culture. Events like the Spiral Tribe parties brought together thousands of people in remote locations, creating a sense of unity and rebellion against the mainstream. French artists like Laurent Garnier, Daft Punk, and Justice took techno to new heights, infusing it with their own artistic vision and pushing boundaries in both production and performance.

Techno also made its mark in other European countries, including the Netherlands, Belgium, Spain, and Italy. Each region developed its own variations and subgenres, contributing to the diverse and ever-evolving European techno landscape. Festivals like Awakenings, Sonar, and Time Warp became annual highlights, attracting techno enthusiasts from all corners of the continent.

The European takeover of techno not only expanded the genre's reach but also brought new perspectives and approaches to its production and performance. The fusion of different cultural influences and artistic sensibilities enriched the techno sound, leading to the emergence of subgenres such as trance, minimal techno, and hard techno.

In the next chapters, we will explore the impact of the Berlin Wall's fall on techno's revolution, the rise of acid house and its influence on UK rave culture, and the crossover hits that propelled techno into the mainstream. Join us as we delve deeper into the fascinating history of techno music and its transformative journey across Europe.

## Chapter 7: The Berlin Wall and Techno's Revolution

The fall of the Berlin Wall in 1989 marked a significant turning point not only in the political history of Germany but also in the evolution of techno music. The dismantling of the wall symbolized the reunification of the city and the liberation of its people, ushering in an era of creative freedom and artistic expression that would profoundly impact the techno scene.

As the barriers came down, a wave of energy swept through Berlin. The city became a blank canvas for cultural experimentation and reinvention. Artists, musicians, and creatives from all over the world flocked to Berlin, drawn by its unique blend of history, opportunity, and artistic openness.

The divided city, which had been a stark symbol of the Cold War, transformed into a playground of possibility. Abandoned buildings, warehouses, and derelict spaces became fertile ground for the emergence of a vibrant underground culture. Techno music found a natural home in this post-wall landscape, providing a soundtrack to the city's rebirth.

One of the most iconic venues to emerge during this period was Tresor. Located in an abandoned department store in the heart of East Berlin, Tresor became the epicenter of the city's burgeoning techno scene. Its gritty atmosphere, pulsating beats, and hedonistic spirit captured the essence of the times, drawing in locals and international visitors alike.

At Tresor and other clubs like E-Werk, Bunker, and Berghain, techno thrived in its rawest and most authentic form. DJs and producers pushed the boundaries, crafting marathon sets that blurred the lines between genres and took dancers on transcendent journeys. The immersive and hedonistic club culture became a symbol of freedom and rebellion against societal norms.

The techno scene in Berlin fostered a sense of community and shared purpose. It brought together people from all walks of life, transcending social, economic, and political divisions. The dancefloor became a space where differences dissolved, and unity prevailed. The shared experience of techno music united a generation, forging connections that went beyond language and nationality.

Techno's revolution in Berlin was not limited to the club scene. It permeated the city's cultural fabric, influencing art, fashion, and even architecture. The city became a living canvas for experimental artists, who drew inspiration from the techno movement's ethos of pushing boundaries and challenging norms. The impact of Berlin's techno revolution reverberated far beyond the city limits. The sound and spirit of Berlin's techno scene inspired countless artists and musicians around the world. It sparked a global fascination with the genre and paved the way for the international recognition of Berlin as a cultural capital.

In the next chapters, we will delve into the impact of acid house on UK rave culture, the rise of techno in the mainstream, and the emergence of techno subgenres. Join us as we continue our journey through the history of techno music, exploring its transformative power and its enduring influence on global culture.

**Chapter 8: The Impact of Acid House: UK Rave Culture**

In the late 1980s, a musical revolution was sweeping across the United Kingdom, and its impact would forever change the course of techno music. This revolution was known as acid house, a subgenre of electronic dance music characterized by its hypnotic beats, squelchy basslines, and mind-altering soundscapes.

Acid house emerged from the underground clubs and warehouse parties of cities like London, Manchester, and Birmingham. It was a reaction against the mainstream music scene and a rebellion against the social and political climate of the time. Acid house provided an escape from the realities of daily life, offering a transformative experience that transcended boundaries and brought people together.

The defining element of acid house was the Roland TB-303 bass synthesizer. Originally designed as a tool for creating basslines, it was repurposed by DJs and producers to generate the signature squelchy, resonant sounds that became synonymous with the genre. The hypnotic, repetitive nature of acid house tracks, combined with the psychedelic and otherworldly sounds of the TB-303, created a sonic journey that captivated audiences.

The 1988 Summer of Love, a series of outdoor rave events held in various locations across the UK, marked the pinnacle of acid house's influence. These massive, unregulated gatherings brought together thousands of like-minded individuals seeking an escape from the constraints of society. Ravers would gather in fields, warehouses, and disused industrial spaces, dancing through the night to the infectious rhythms of acid house.

The impact of acid house on UK rave culture cannot be overstated. It was more than just a genre of music; it was a cultural phenomenon that challenged conventions and fostered a sense of unity and togetherness. Rave culture became a movement, with its distinctive fashion, iconography, and values of peace, love, unity, and respect.

The illegal nature of many acid house events and the authorities' attempts to shut them down only added fuel to the fire. Ravers were relentless in their pursuit of the next party, using secret locations, word-of-mouth communication, and an unwavering determination to keep the movement alive.

The popularity of acid house spilled over into the mainstream, with chart-topping hits such as "Voodoo Ray" by A Guy Called Gerald and "Pacific State" by 808 State. These crossover successes brought the sound of acid house to a wider audience, introducing them to the infectious rhythms and euphoric energy that had captivated underground ravers.

The legacy of acid house continues to reverberate in the UK and beyond. It laid the groundwork for the subsequent development of electronic dance music, influencing genres such as techno, trance, and house. The spirit of rave culture lives on in the countless festivals, club nights, and events that celebrate the power of music and bring people together in joyous unity.

In the next chapters, we will explore the mainstream success of techno, the rise of techno subgenres, and the global impact of techno music. Join us as we continue our journey through the history of techno, tracing its evolution and uncovering its profound influence on the world of music and beyond.

## Chapter 9: Techno in the Mainstream: Pop Crossover Hits

As techno music continued to evolve and capture the hearts of music lovers, it began to make its way into the mainstream. The infectious beats, pulsating rhythms, and futuristic sounds of techno found their way onto radio airwaves, music charts, and even television.

One of the key moments that brought techno into the mainstream was the release of "Pump Up the Jam" by Technotronic in 1989. This iconic track fused elements of hip-hop, house, and techno, creating a catchy and energetic anthem that resonated with audiences worldwide. "Pump Up the Jam" became a global hit, reaching the top of the charts in multiple countries and introducing many people to the sound and energy of techno.

The success of "Pump Up the Jam" opened the floodgates for other techno-infused pop crossover hits. Artists like Snap! with their song "Rhythm Is a Dancer" and 2 Unlimited with their track "No Limit" brought techno influences into the mainstream pop music landscape. These songs were characterized by their infectious hooks, driving beats, and catchy melodies, making them instant favorites on dance floors and radio stations alike.

Techno's popularity in the mainstream also led to the emergence of techno-inspired dance routines and choreographies. From music videos to live performances, artists and dancers incorporated techno-inspired moves, robotic gestures, and synchronized routines that reflected the mechanical and futuristic nature of the music. The visual spectacle of techno-infused performances added another dimension to the genre's appeal, captivating audiences with a combination of sound and movement.

The rise of techno in the mainstream also sparked the interest of major record labels and music producers. They saw the commercial potential of techno and sought to capitalize on its growing popularity. As a result, techno tracks were remixed, repackaged, and marketed to a broader audience. The remix culture surrounding techno allowed for reinterpretations and adaptations of the genre, blending it with other styles and genres to create unique and accessible versions of techno for mainstream consumption.

The influence of techno in the mainstream extended beyond the charts and dance floors. Techno-inspired fashion trends emerged, with bold colors, metallic fabrics, and futuristic designs becoming popular among trendsetters and fashion-forward individuals. The distinctive aesthetic of techno culture influenced not only clothing but also hairstyles, accessories, and even interior design, reflecting the sleek and futuristic sensibilities of the genre.

While techno's journey into the mainstream brought it increased exposure and commercial success, it also raised debates among purists and critics who questioned whether the genre's essence was being diluted or compromised. Some argued that the mainstream appropriation of techno diminished its underground origins and rebellious spirit, while others embraced the idea of techno reaching a wider audience and evolving in new and exciting directions. Regardless of the debates surrounding its mainstream success, techno's foray into pop crossover hits marked a significant milestone in the genre's history. It showcased the versatility and adaptability of techno music, proving that its infectious beats and futuristic sounds could captivate audiences beyond the confines of underground clubs and raves.

In the following chapters, we will explore the diverse subgenres that emerged within the techno realm, the global influence of techno on electronic music, and the transformative impact of techno in the digital age. Join us as we continue our journey through the vibrant and ever-evolving history of techno music.

## Chapter 10: Techno Subgenres: Ambient, Industrial, and Hardcore

Techno music has always been a fertile ground for experimentation and innovation, leading to the emergence of various subgenres that pushed the boundaries of the genre even further. In this chapter, we will explore three prominent techno subgenres: ambient techno, industrial techno, and hardcore techno.

Ambient Techno: Ambient techno combines the atmospheric, ethereal elements of ambient music with the driving beats and pulsating rhythms of techno. It creates a sonic landscape that is both hypnotic and introspective. Artists like Aphex Twin, The Orb, and Biosphere are known for their contributions to ambient techno, creating immersive soundscapes that transport listeners to otherworldly realms.

Industrial Techno: Industrial techno draws inspiration from the harsh and mechanical sounds of industrial music. It incorporates aggressive percussion, distorted synths, and abrasive textures to create a dark and intense sonic experience. Artists such as Ancient Methods, Perc, and Blawan are known for their exploration of industrial techno, injecting raw energy and a dystopian atmosphere into their compositions.

Hardcore Techno: Hardcore techno, also known as gabber, emerged in the early 1990s as a high-energy and frenetic subgenre of techno. It is characterized by its fast tempo, pounding kick drums, and aggressive synthesizer sounds. Hardcore techno often features distorted vocals and samples, creating an intense and relentless sonic assault. Artists like DJ Paul Elstak, The Prophet, and Neophyte played a pivotal role in popularizing hardcore techno and establishing it as a distinct subgenre within the techno scene.

These techno subgenres represent the diverse directions that artists have taken within the broader techno landscape. They showcase the genre's ability to evolve, adapt, and incorporate different influences, resulting in unique and innovative sonic experiences.

## Chapter 11: Techno Goes Global: Influence on Electronic Music Worldwide

Techno music has transcended borders and gained a global following, leaving an indelible mark on electronic music scenes worldwide. From Detroit's birthplace to cities like Berlin, London, Amsterdam, and beyond, techno has become a driving force in shaping electronic music cultures across the globe. The spread of techno music can be attributed to several factors. Firstly, advancements in technology and the internet have made it easier for artists to connect, collaborate, and share their music globally. Online platforms, social media, and streaming services have provided a platform for artists to reach international audiences, breaking down geographical barriers and facilitating the dissemination of techno music.

Secondly, the influence of techno festivals and events cannot be overlooked. From legendary festivals like Detroit's Movement Electronic Music Festival to Amsterdam's Awakenings and Berlin's Berghain, these events have become meccas for techno enthusiasts, drawing crowds from all corners of the world. Techno festivals offer a unique experience, combining music, art installations, immersive environments, and a sense of community, further fueling the global appeal of the genre.

Techno's influence on electronic music scenes worldwide is evident in the emergence of local scenes and subcultures that have embraced and adapted the genre to their own cultural contexts. For example, in Brazil, the fusion of techno with local rhythms and sounds has given rise to the genre known as "Brazilian techno" or "Brazilian tech-house," creating a unique blend of traditional and electronic music elements.

In Japan, the influence of techno can be seen in the vibrant and innovative electronic music scene, with artists like Ken Ishii and Takkyu Ishino gaining international recognition for their contributions to the genre. Similarly, in Australia, the underground techno scene has thrived, with cities like Melbourne and Sydney becoming hotspots for techno enthusiasts and showcasing local talents.

Techno's global reach has also led to cross-pollination and collaboration between artists from different countries and backgrounds. International DJ tours, label partnerships, and remix exchanges have become commonplace, allowing artists to exchange ideas, share their musical perspectives, and contribute to the evolution of techno as a global phenomenon.
In the next chapter, we will delve into the impact of the digital age on techno music, exploring how the rise of digital technologies, software, and online platforms have transformed the way techno is produced, distributed, and consumed. Join us as we uncover the revolutionary changes that have shaped the techno landscape in the 21st century.

## Chapter 12: Techno in the Digital Age: The Rise of DJs and Producers

The digital age has revolutionized the way music is created, produced, and consumed, and techno music has not been immune to these transformative changes. In this chapter, we will explore the impact of digital technologies on the techno scene, focusing on the rise of DJs and producers who have embraced these tools to shape the genre's sound and reach wider audiences. One of the most significant changes brought about by the digital age is the accessibility and affordability of music production tools. In the past, producing techno music required expensive hardware, such as synthesizers, drum machines, and samplers. Today, aspiring techno producers can create entire tracks using software-based digital audio workstations (DAWs) and a laptop. This democratization of music production has allowed a new generation of artists to enter the techno scene, unleashing a wave of creativity and diversity. Digital DJing has also played a pivotal role in the evolution of techno. With the advent of DJ software, controllers, and digital media players, DJs have been able to carry extensive music libraries in a compact format and perform intricate mixes with precise control. The transition from vinyl to digital formats has made DJing more accessible and convenient, enabling DJs to explore a broader range of musical styles, experiment with live remixing and looping, and create seamless sets that push the boundaries of traditional DJ performances.

Furthermore, the internet and online platforms have transformed the way techno music is discovered, shared, and consumed. Online music stores, streaming services, and digital platforms have become the primary channels for accessing and distributing techno music. Artists can independently release their tracks, connect with fans through social media, and reach global audiences without relying on traditional record labels or physical distribution channels.

The rise of social media has also had a profound impact on the techno community. Artists, labels, and promoters can engage with fans directly, share updates, and promote events, fostering a sense of community and interconnectedness. Online communities, forums, and music-sharing platforms have facilitated the exchange of ideas, feedback, and collaborations, allowing artists to connect and collaborate across borders and continents.

While the digital age has brought numerous benefits to the techno scene, it has also raised questions and challenges. The ease of digital production and distribution has led to a saturation of music releases, making it increasingly difficult for artists to stand out in a crowded market. The emphasis on online presence and social media can sometimes overshadow the importance of the music itself, shifting the focus towards branding and visibility rather than artistic expression.

In the following chapters, we will explore techno as a form of resistance, its impact on political and social movements, the vibrant culture of techno festivals and raving, and the future directions of techno music. Join us as we delve deeper into the multifaceted world of techno and its ongoing evolution in the digital age.

## Chapter 13: Techno as Resistance: Political and Social Movements

Techno music has often served as a powerful platform for expressing dissent, challenging social norms, and advocating for change. In this chapter, we will explore how techno has been intertwined with political and social movements, becoming a form of resistance and a catalyst for social transformation. Throughout history, techno has been embraced by marginalized communities and individuals who have used it as a means of self-expression and empowerment. In cities like Detroit, techno music emerged as a response to the economic decline and racial tensions, providing an outlet for creativity and a way to reclaim spaces that had been neglected by mainstream society. The Belleville Three, along with other artists and promoters, played a crucial role in establishing a thriving techno scene in Detroit, giving voice to the aspirations and frustrations of the city's African American community.

Techno's association with social and political movements became more pronounced in the 1990s, particularly in Europe. In Berlin, techno music became intertwined with the spirit of reunification following the fall of the Berlin Wall. Abandoned buildings and warehouses became the birthplace of underground techno parties, where people from both sides of the wall came together to dance, celebrate, and challenge the status quo. Techno raves became a symbol of unity, breaking down barriers and fostering a sense of collective consciousness.

Beyond its symbolic significance, techno music has also been a driving force behind activist movements. In the late 1980s and early 1990s, the Spiral Tribe collective in the UK organized illegal raves in protest against restrictive government policies on party culture and civil liberties. These "free parties" became sites of resistance, where participants championed the principles of freedom, equality, and autonomy.

Techno's rebellious spirit has continued to inspire and shape contemporary social and political movements. In recent years, techno has been embraced by LGBTQ+ communities as a means of self-expression, empowerment, and resistance against discrimination. Techno clubs and events have provided safe spaces for individuals to explore their identities, challenge societal norms, and build supportive communities.

Furthermore, techno has also been a platform for advocating environmental sustainability and raising awareness about pressing ecological issues. Festivals and events have incorporated sustainable practices, such as renewable energy sources, waste reduction, and eco-conscious initiatives, to promote a greener and more responsible techno culture.

As we delve into the diverse and dynamic intersections between techno music and political/social movements, we will uncover stories of resilience, defiance, and collective action. From Detroit to Berlin, from underground parties to mainstream festivals, techno's role as a form of resistance continues to evolve, inspiring individuals to challenge the status quo and imagine alternative futures.

## Chapter 14: Techno Festivals and the Culture of Raving

Techno music and festivals have become inseparable, with the vibrant and immersive experiences of raving playing a significant role in shaping the culture surrounding the genre. In this chapter, we will explore the evolution of techno festivals, their cultural impact, and the unique experiences they offer to participants.

Techno festivals provide a space for techno enthusiasts to come together, celebrate the music, and immerse themselves in a sensory journey. These events are more than just concerts; they are multi-day experiences that blend music, art installations, visuals, performance art, and interactive experiences. From large-scale festivals like Awakenings, Time Warp, and Movement Electronic Music Festival to smaller, niche gatherings, techno festivals offer a range of experiences catering to different tastes and preferences.

One of the defining features of techno festivals is their emphasis on community and inclusivity. Participants from diverse backgrounds come together, united by their love for the music and the shared experience of raving. The sense of belonging and connection fostered at these festivals has led to the formation of tight-knit communities and lasting friendships.

Techno festivals also provide a platform for showcasing emerging talent and established artists, creating opportunities for discovery and supporting the growth of the techno scene. The lineup at techno festivals often features a mix of local and international artists, representing different styles and subgenres within the broader techno spectrum. From headliners to underground acts, these festivals offer a diverse range of musical journeys, allowing attendees to explore new sounds and connect with their favorite artists.

Beyond the music, techno festivals often incorporate visual and immersive elements to enhance the overall experience. Mind-bending visuals, stage designs, light shows, and art installations create an otherworldly atmosphere, blurring the boundaries between reality and fantasy. The combination of sound and visuals creates a multi-sensory experience that transports participants into a different realm, amplifying the euphoria and energy of the music.

Techno festivals are also known for their dedication to creating safe and inclusive spaces. Event organizers prioritize participant well-being by implementing harm reduction measures, providing medical services, and promoting consent and respect within the festival environment. Creating a culture of inclusivity and respect is central to the techno festival ethos, ensuring that everyone feels welcome and can fully enjoy the experience without fear of discrimination or harassment.

In the final chapter of our journey through the history of techno music, we will explore the future visions and the evolution of techno. We will examine how the genre continues to evolve, adapt to new technological advancements, and push the boundaries of artistic expression. Join us as we delve into the ever-changing landscape of techno music and its limitless potential.

## Chapter 15: Future Visions: The Evolution of Techno Music

Techno music has always been characterized by its forward-thinking nature, constantly evolving and reinventing itself. In this final chapter, we will explore the future visions of techno and the ways in which the genre continues to push boundaries, challenge conventions, and embrace innovation.

As we enter the digital age, techno music finds itself at the forefront of technological advancements. From new production techniques to innovative live performance setups, artists are constantly exploring new ways to create and present their music. The integration of artificial intelligence, machine learning, and virtual reality has opened up exciting possibilities for the future of techno, allowing artists to push the boundaries of sound design and create immersive experiences for listeners.

The rise of streaming platforms and online communities has democratized access to techno music, making it more accessible to a global audience. Artists are no longer limited to physical record releases or traditional distribution channels; they can independently release their music, connect with fans directly, and experiment with new business models. The internet has become a breeding ground for innovation and collaboration, enabling artists to reach new audiences, collaborate with like-minded creators, and explore new sonic territories.

Furthermore, the boundaries between genres continue to blur, with techno artists incorporating elements from diverse musical styles and traditions. Experimental techno, ambient techno, and industrial techno are just a few examples of subgenres that have emerged, expanding the sonic palette and pushing the genre into new directions. Techno artists are also embracing hybrid live performances, incorporating live instruments, vocals, and visuals into their sets, creating truly immersive and unique experiences.

The future of techno is also shaped by the socio-political context in which it exists. Techno has always been closely intertwined with societal movements and cultural shifts, and this will continue to influence its trajectory. As we navigate through an increasingly interconnected and complex world, techno music has the potential to serve as a form of commentary, a channel for expressing collective anxieties and aspirations, and a platform for fostering unity and empathy.

In conclusion, the history of techno music is a testament to its enduring impact and cultural significance. From its humble beginnings in Detroit to its global reach today, techno has transformed the musical landscape and continues to evolve, adapt, and inspire. By exploring its origins, pioneers, subgenres, cultural movements, and future visions, we gain a deeper appreciation for the rich tapestry of sound, creativity, and human expression that is techno music. As we move forward, let us embrace the rhythms of the future and celebrate the unifying power of techno.

The current techno scene in London is a vibrant and dynamic landscape that continues to thrive and evolve. Known for its diverse and influential music culture, the city has been a hotbed for techno enthusiasts, artists, and underground parties for decades.

London's techno scene offers a wide range of experiences, from intimate warehouse raves to larger-scale club nights and festivals. It boasts a multitude of venues that cater to techno enthusiasts, each with its own unique atmosphere and sonic identity. From iconic establishments like fabric, Corsica Studios, and Village Underground to smaller, more clandestine spaces, there is a venue to suit every taste and preference.

One of the defining features of London's techno scene is its inclusivity and openness to experimentation. The city has long been a melting pot of cultures and influences, and this is reflected in its techno community. Artists from various backgrounds and genres come together to push the boundaries of techno, blending it with elements of house, electro, acid, and more. This fusion of styles creates a dynamic and eclectic sound that is distinctly London. In recent years, London has seen a resurgence of interest in the underground techno scene. A new generation of promoters, collectives, and artists has emerged, bringing fresh energy and innovation to the city's nightlife. These individuals are dedicated to creating unique experiences for techno enthusiasts, often organizing events in unconventional spaces like warehouses, lofts, and outdoor locations. The underground nature of these parties fosters a sense of intimacy and connection among attendees, allowing for a more immersive and authentic techno experience.

Beyond the club scene, London also hosts a number of techno-focused festivals and events that attract both local and international talent. Events like Junction 2, Printworks, and LWE regularly showcase some of the biggest names in techno, while also providing a platform for emerging artists to shine. These festivals offer a full sensory experience, combining cutting-edge production, immersive visuals, and carefully curated lineups to create unforgettable moments for attendees.

The current techno scene in London is also characterized by its strong sense of community and collaboration. Artists, promoters, and techno enthusiasts come together to support each other, fostering a supportive network that encourages creativity and artistic growth. This collaborative spirit can be seen in the various artist collectives and labels that have emerged, working together to release music, organize events, and champion the city's techno talent.

However, it is important to note that the techno scene in London, like in any city, faces its own set of challenges. Rising rent prices, increasing regulations, and gentrification pose threats to the underground culture that has been at the heart of London's techno scene. Nonetheless, the resilience and passion of the community continue to drive the scene forward, adapting to these challenges and finding new ways to keep the spirit of techno alive.

In conclusion, the current techno scene in London is a vibrant and ever-evolving ecosystem that celebrates diversity, experimentation, and inclusivity. It serves as a testament to the enduring power of techno music as a force of cultural expression and connection. Whether you're a seasoned techno enthusiast or a curious newcomer, London offers a plethora of experiences and opportunities to immerse yourself in the pulsating rhythms and electrifying energy of the city's techno scene.

The techno scene in Brighton is currently pulsating with energy and creativity, establishing itself as a thriving hub for electronic music enthusiasts. Known for its vibrant nightlife and alternative culture, Brighton offers a unique and eclectic techno experience that attracts both local talent and international artists.

The city boasts a diverse range of venues that cater to techno aficionados, from intimate basement clubs to larger warehouse spaces. Renowned establishments such as Patterns, The Arch, and Hideout provide immersive environments where techno enthusiasts can lose themselves in the infectious beats and hypnotic rhythms of the genre. These venues often host both established techno artists and up-and-coming talent, fostering a sense of discovery and excitement among attendees.

Brighton's techno scene prides itself on its forward-thinking approach, embracing a wide spectrum of subgenres and experimental sounds. From deep and dubby techno to driving and industrial rhythms, there is something to cater to every musical taste. The scene thrives on diversity and welcomes artists who push the boundaries of traditional techno, incorporating elements from other genres and embracing innovative production techniques.

Beyond the club environment, Brighton's techno community is known for its collaborative spirit and DIY ethos. Independent promoters and collectives play a crucial role in organizing underground parties and events, often in unconventional spaces such as art galleries, warehouses, and outdoor locations. These events offer a more intimate and immersive experience, allowing attendees to connect with the music and each other on a deeper level.

Brighton also hosts several techno-focused festivals and events throughout the year, drawing crowds from both near and far. The likes of Concorde 2, Boundary Brighton, and The Arch frequently showcase a diverse lineup of established techno artists, alongside local talent, creating a vibrant and inclusive festival atmosphere. These events not only contribute to the city's cultural fabric but also provide platforms for emerging artists to gain exposure and showcase their unique sound.

The techno scene in Brighton is deeply rooted in community and collaboration. Local DJs, producers, and promoters support each other, fostering a nurturing environment for artistic growth and exploration. The scene is driven by a passion for music and a shared love for the underground, creating a sense of unity and belonging among its participants.

Moreover, Brighton's techno scene is not limited to the nightlife. The city embraces a broader cultural appreciation for electronic music, with music academies, workshops, and talks offering opportunities for aspiring DJs and producers to learn and connect with industry professionals. This commitment to education and skill-sharing contributes to the scene's continuous growth and evolution.

In conclusion, the techno scene in Brighton is a dynamic and diverse community that thrives on innovation, collaboration, and a deep appreciation for electronic music. With its eclectic mix of venues, forward-thinking artists, and inclusive events, Brighton has solidified its place as a haven for techno enthusiasts. Whether you're seeking an intimate underground experience or a pulsating festival atmosphere, Brighton's techno scene promises to deliver unforgettable moments and a vibrant celebration of electronic music culture.

The best techno location today is undoubtedly Berlin, Germany. Renowned worldwide for its thriving electronic music scene, Berlin has cemented its position as a mecca for techno enthusiasts and artists alike.
Berlin's techno landscape offers a multitude of venues that cater specifically to the genre, providing immersive and unparalleled experiences for music lovers. From legendary clubs such as Berghain, Tresor, and Watergate to smaller, more intimate spaces like Salon zur & Wilden Renate the city offers a diverse range of environments where techno enthusiasts can immerse themselves in the pulsating rhythms and hypnotic beats.

One of the factors that sets Berlin apart as a techno destination is its 24/7 party culture. Many of the city's renowned clubs operate throughout the weekend, often starting on Friday evening and continuing non-stop until Monday morning or even later. This unique feature allows partygoers to fully immerse themselves in the music, with marathon sessions lasting for hours or even days.

Berlin's techno scene is characterized by its openness and inclusivity, welcoming both established artists and emerging talent from around the globe. The city has served as a platform for countless DJs, producers, and live acts to showcase their skills and push the boundaries of the genre. The diverse range of artists and styles represented in Berlin's techno scene ensures a rich and ever-evolving sonic landscape.

In addition to its world-class clubs, Berlin hosts numerous techno-focused events and festivals throughout the year. From the iconic Love Parade that once attracted hundreds of thousands of people to the city's streets to more intimate gatherings like the CTM Festival and the Krake Festival, there is always an event or festival showcasing cutting-edge techno music and immersive experiences.

Beyond the nightlife, Berlin's techno culture extends into other realms of creative expression. The city is home to a thriving community of artists, designers, and collectives who collaborate to create immersive audio-visual experiences, combining innovative visuals with powerful techno soundscapes. The city's commitment to the arts and creativity is evident in its numerous galleries, street art, and cultural spaces that serve as platforms for experimentation and collaboration.

Moreover, Berlin's techno scene has a profound influence on global electronic music culture. The city's sound has shaped and influenced countless artists, labels, and subgenres, spreading its influence to every corner of the globe. Techno enthusiasts and aspiring artists flock to Berlin to immerse themselves in its unique atmosphere and to tap into the creative energy that flows through the city's veins.

In conclusion, Berlin stands as the best techno location today, offering a thriving and diverse ecosystem for techno enthusiasts and artists. With its legendary clubs, 24/7 party culture, cutting-edge events, and global influence, Berlin continues to set the bar for techno excellence. It remains a pilgrimage site for electronic music lovers, a place where the spirit of techno thrives and continues to shape the future of the genre.

Techno has remained a popular genre of electronic music since its inception in the early 1980s, but its popularity and influence have certainly evolved over time. In the early 90s, techno experienced a surge in popularity and reached a peak in mainstream recognition and cultural impact.

During the early 90s, techno music gained significant traction in various parts of the world, particularly in Europe and the United States. It became synonymous with the rave culture and the emergence of electronic dance music as a global phenomenon. The energetic beats, hypnotic melodies, and futuristic soundscapes of techno captivated audiences and created a sense of unity and euphoria on dance floors.

At that time, techno was not only popular among underground music enthusiasts but also attracted mainstream attention. Techno tracks started to infiltrate the charts and radio airwaves, and techno artists achieved commercial success and recognition. Genres like techno-pop and Eurodance emerged, blending techno elements with catchy melodies and pop sensibilities, further contributing to its popularity.

In the early 90s, large-scale techno events and festivals, such as the Love Parade in Berlin and the Mayday Festival in Germany, drew massive crowds, showcasing the genre's immense appeal. These events became cultural phenomena, attracting hundreds of thousands of attendees and solidifying techno's place in the global music landscape.

Fast forward to today, techno continues to be a prominent force in the electronic music scene, although its mainstream popularity may have waned slightly compared to the early 90s. Techno has become more specialized, often finding its home in underground clubs, festivals, and niche electronic music scenes.

While techno may not dominate the mainstream charts as it did in the early 90s, it maintains a dedicated and passionate following around the world. The underground techno community remains vibrant and active, with a plethora of talented artists, labels, and promoters pushing the boundaries of the genre.

Moreover, the digital age and the rise of streaming platforms have made it easier for techno enthusiasts to discover and explore a vast array of techno subgenres and artists. Techno has also found new avenues of expression through the proliferation of online radio stations, podcasts, and curated playlists, further fueling its reach and influence.

In summary, while the popularity of techno may have shifted over the years, it remains a significant and influential genre in the electronic music landscape. Its early 90s heyday brought it widespread recognition and mainstream success, but today it continues to thrive as a beloved and celebrated genre within dedicated communities, ensuring its lasting impact on the global music scene.

## Nina Kraviz: A Journey Through Sonic Realms

Nina Kraviz, a name that reverberates throughout the techno landscape, emerged as a force to be reckoned with in the global electronic music scene. Hailing from Irkutsk, Siberia, she embarked on an extraordinary journey that would see her conquer dance floors worldwide and leave an indelible mark on the genre she holds so dear.

Nina's story begins in the unassuming town of Irkutsk, where her love affair with music was ignited at a young age. Surrounded by the enchanting beauty of the Siberian wilderness, she found solace in the melodic sounds that transported her beyond the confines of her humble surroundings. Drawn to the world of electronic music, Nina's curiosity led her on a path of discovery, where she unearthed the pulsating rhythms and mesmerizing beats of techno.

As her passion grew, Nina found herself irresistibly drawn to the allure of the DJ booth. Armed with an insatiable thirst for sonic exploration, she honed her skills behind the decks, delving deep into the realms of vinyl and embracing the art of mixing. It was here that she discovered her innate ability to weave together disparate sounds and genres, crafting sets that seamlessly fused the ethereal with the raw.

With her unwavering dedication and innate talent, Nina's reputation began to spread like wildfire. Her name became synonymous with electrifying performances that transcended the boundaries of traditional DJ sets. As she stepped onto the stage, a surge of energy filled the room, anticipation hung in the air, and the crowd prepared for a sonic journey unlike any other.

Nina's style was a tapestry of emotions, effortlessly shifting between deep, hypnotic grooves and relentless beats that sent shivers down spines. Her ability to connect with the audience was unparalleled, drawing them into a transcendent state where time seemed to stand still. The dance floor became a sanctuary, a place where bodies moved in harmony, and souls were liberated by the power of music.

As her star ascended, Nina's creative vision expanded beyond the confines of the DJ booth. She ventured into the realm of production, crafting tracks that echoed the depths of her musical soul. Her releases on revered labels like

Rekids and Trip showcased her versatility, effortlessly traversing sonic landscapes and pushing the boundaries of the genre.

But Nina's journey didn't end there. Fuelled by an unyielding desire to shape the future of techno, she founded her own record label, imprinting her unique vision onto the industry. Her label became a platform for emerging talents, a haven where sonic pioneers could flourish and unleash their creative potential.

Beyond the music, Nina's enigmatic presence became an inspiration for aspiring artists and a beacon of empowerment for women in the male-dominated world of electronic music. Her success served as a testament to the power of determination, resilience, and the unrelenting pursuit of one's passions.

Today, Nina Kraviz stands as a luminary, a trailblazer who continues to push boundaries and challenge conventions. Her sonic explorations have become a soundtrack for countless journeys of self-discovery and liberation. Whether performing on iconic stages, curating unforgettable experiences, or sharing her knowledge through mentorship, Nina remains an unwavering force driving techno forward.

In the vast tapestry of electronic music, Nina Kraviz has woven her own chapter, a testament to the transformative power of music and the boundless potential of those who dare to dream. As her journey continues to unfold, one thing is certain: Nina Kraviz will forever be an icon, a guiding light in the realm of techno, shaping the future with her unwavering passion and unparalleled talent.

## Adam Beyer: The Swedish Techno Titan

Born and raised in Stockholm, Sweden, Adam Beyer has emerged as a true force within the global techno scene. With his unwavering dedication to the genre and his unparalleled talent, Beyer has become a symbol of innovation and inspiration for techno enthusiasts around the world.

Beyer's love affair with electronic music began at a young age, fueled by his fascination with the boundless possibilities of sound. It was in the late 1980s that he discovered the raw, hypnotic beats of techno, a genre that would come to define his artistic journey.

In the early days of his career, Beyer honed his skills as a DJ, immersing himself in the vibrant club culture of Stockholm. Drawing inspiration from the likes of Jeff Mills and Richie Hawtin, he began to develop his unique sound, a perfect balance of driving rhythms, atmospheric textures, and captivating melodies.

As Beyer's reputation grew, he found himself at the forefront of the techno movement. In 1996, he established Drumcode, a record label that would become synonymous with cutting-edge techno releases. Through Drumcode, Beyer has nurtured a roster of talented artists, providing them with a platform to showcase their creativity and push the boundaries of the genre.

Beyer's productions are a testament to his meticulous craftsmanship and his ability to create immersive sonic experiences. His tracks, such as "Your Mind" and "Stone Flower," have become modern classics, revered for their infectious energy and expertly crafted soundscapes. With each release, Beyer pushes the boundaries of his own artistry, constantly evolving and reinventing his sound.

But it is Beyer's DJ sets that truly showcase his genius. Armed with a vast knowledge of music and an innate ability to read the crowd, he weaves together a tapestry of sounds that takes listeners on a journey of epic proportions. From the dark and brooding depths to the euphoric peaks, Beyer's sets are a masterclass in storytelling and a testament to the power of music to transcend boundaries.

Beyond his own artistic endeavors, Beyer has played a pivotal role in shaping the global techno community. His appearances at major festivals and iconic venues have brought his unique vision to audiences around the world, leaving an indelible mark on the hearts and minds of techno enthusiasts.

Adam Beyer's impact on the techno scene cannot be overstated. His relentless pursuit of excellence, his commitment to pushing boundaries, and his passion for the music have made him a true icon in the world of electronic music. As techno continues to evolve and thrive, Beyer remains at the forefront, constantly innovating and inspiring the next generation of artists and music lovers.

In the ever-changing landscape of electronic music, Adam Beyer stands tall as a guiding light, a visionary artist who has left an indelible mark on the genre and continues to shape its future. With his unwavering dedication to his craft and his unwavering commitment to pushing boundaries, Beyer's influence will undoubtedly continue to resonate for years to come.

## Amelie Lens: The Belgian Techno Powerhouse

Amelie Lens, the rising star from Belgium, has taken the techno scene by storm with her electrifying performances and a distinct musical style that sets her apart from the rest. With her unwavering passion for techno and an innate ability to connect with audiences, Lens has quickly become one of the most sought-after DJs and producers in the industry.

Hailing from Antwerp, Belgium, Lens was drawn to electronic music from an early age. Inspired by the pulsating beats and hypnotic rhythms of techno, she embarked on a musical journey that would lead her to global recognition. Lens' dedication to her craft and her meticulous attention to detail are evident in every aspect of her work.

Lens' DJ sets are a masterclass in energy and intensity. Known for her seamless mixing and impeccable track selection, she effortlessly guides her audience through a sonic journey that spans the entire spectrum of techno. From deep and atmospheric grooves to pounding basslines and driving beats, Lens' sets are a rollercoaster of emotions that leave crowds mesmerized and hungry for more.

In addition to her exceptional DJ skills, Lens has also made a mark as a producer. Her releases on esteemed labels such as Lenske and Second State have garnered critical acclaim, showcasing her ability to craft powerful, dancefloor-oriented tracks that push the boundaries of the genre. Lens' production style is characterized by its raw energy, dark atmospheres, and a relentless drive that captivates listeners from start to finish.

One of the defining features of Lens' career is her unwavering dedication to the techno community. She has used her platform to support emerging artists and champion their music, curating events and showcases that shine a spotlight on rising talents. Lens' commitment to nurturing the next generation of techno artists demonstrates her passion for the genre and her desire to see it flourish.

Lens' meteoric rise to prominence has seen her perform at some of the world's most prestigious venues and festivals. From intimate club shows to massive outdoor stages, she commands the crowd with her infectious energy and infectious beats. Her ability to connect with her audience on a deep and personal level is a testament to her talent and charisma.

As Amelie Lens continues to push boundaries and inspire others with her music, she remains a beacon of innovation and passion in the techno world. Her relentless pursuit of excellence, coupled with her unwavering love for the genre, sets her apart as a true force to be reckoned with. With each performance, Lens solidifies her position as a leading figure in the global techno scene, leaving an indelible mark on the hearts and minds of techno enthusiasts worldwide.

## Charlotte de Witte: The Belgian Techno Sensation

Charlotte de Witte has established herself as one of the most prominent figures in the contemporary techno landscape. Hailing from Belgium, this talented DJ and producer has garnered widespread acclaim for her unique style and captivating performances. With her infectious energy and uncompromising dedication to techno, de Witte has carved a distinct path for herself in the electronic music scene.

Born and raised in Ghent, Belgium, de Witte's love affair with music began at a young age. Influenced by her father, a connoisseur of vinyl records, she developed a deep appreciation for various genres. However, it was the allure of techno that truly captivated her. De Witte was drawn to its dark, driving beats and its ability to create a sense of unity on the dancefloor.

Driven by her passion, de Witte embarked on a journey to master her craft. She spent countless hours refining her DJing skills and honing her own sound. It wasn't long before she caught the attention of industry insiders, and her career took off at a rapid pace.

Known for her captivating DJ sets, de Witte effortlessly weaves together a sonic tapestry that blurs the lines between genres. Her performances are characterized by relentless energy, seamless transitions, and carefully curated track selections that keep audiences on their toes. Whether she's playing in intimate clubs or commanding massive festival stages, de Witte's stage presence is magnetic, drawing crowds into a euphoric techno trance.

In addition to her DJing prowess, de Witte has made waves as a producer. Her releases on renowned labels like KNTXT and NovaMute have garnered critical acclaim and solidified her position as a driving force in the studio as well. Her productions are characterized by their powerful basslines, hypnotic melodies, and atmospheric textures, showcasing her ability to create immersive sonic experiences that transport listeners to another realm.

Beyond her musical talents, de Witte has also been recognized for her entrepreneurial spirit. In 2017, she launched her own label, KNTXT, providing a platform for her own releases as well as showcasing emerging talents in the techno realm. The label has quickly gained a reputation for its uncompromising quality and innovative sound, further establishing de Witte as a tastemaker and visionary in the industry.

As Charlotte de Witte continues to push boundaries and captivate audiences with her unparalleled talent, she remains a driving force in the evolution of techno. Her passion for the music, combined with her technical prowess and unique artistic vision, sets her apart as an artist who is constantly pushing the genre forward. With each performance and production, de Witte solidifies her status as a true techno sensation, leaving an indelible mark on the hearts and minds of electronic music lovers worldwide.

## Ben Klock: The Techno Maestro

Ben Klock stands as one of the most influential figures in the world of techno. With his impeccable mixing skills, meticulous attention to detail, and a deep understanding of the genre, Klock has earned a reputation as a true maestro of techno. Hailing from Berlin, Germany, he has played a pivotal role in shaping the city's renowned techno scene and has become a global icon in the process.

From his early days as a resident DJ at the renowned Berghain nightclub to his countless international performances, Klock has consistently captivated audiences with his hypnotic and driving sound. His DJ sets are a masterclass in seamless mixing, blending together a diverse range of tracks to create a cohesive and immersive experience. With a keen sense of timing and an instinctive ability to read the crowd, Klock builds tension and energy on the dancefloor, taking listeners on a journey through the depths of techno.

Beyond his extraordinary DJ skills, Klock has also made a significant impact as a producer. His releases on his own label, Klockworks, have become synonymous with quality and innovation in the techno world. His productions are characterized by their pulsating basslines, intricate percussion, and atmospheric textures, creating a distinct and hypnotic sound that resonates with listeners worldwide. Klock's music strikes a balance between raw power and introspective depth, immersing listeners in a sonic landscape that transcends the boundaries of traditional techno.

Klock's contributions to the techno community extend beyond his own performances and productions. He has been instrumental in nurturing and supporting emerging talent through his work as a mentor and curator. With his passion for pushing the boundaries of techno and his commitment to showcasing new voices, Klock has played a vital role in shaping the future of the genre.

In addition to his solo endeavors, Klock is also known for his collaboration with fellow techno luminary Marcel Dettmann. Together, they have formed a powerful partnership, both as DJs and producers, releasing a series of highly acclaimed mixes and EPs that showcase their shared vision for techno's evolution.

As Ben Klock continues to push the boundaries of techno and inspire generations of artists and fans alike, his impact on the genre cannot be overstated. His unwavering dedication, technical brilliance, and ability to create transcendent musical experiences have solidified his place as one of the most respected and revered figures in techno. With each performance, Klock reaffirms his status as a true maestro, guiding the global techno community into new realms of sonic exploration.

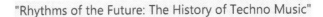

## Jack Anarchy: The Rebel of Techno

Jack Anarchy is a name that has become synonymous with rebellion and non-conformity in the world of techno. With his bold style, provocative performances, and boundary-pushing music, Anarchy has carved out a unique place for himself in the electronic music landscape. Born out of a desire to challenge the status quo, his artistic vision is fueled by a rebellious spirit that seeks to break free from the constraints of convention.

Hailing from a small town in the underground scene, Anarchy's journey began with a deep love for music and a burning desire to create something truly different. He was drawn to the raw energy and rebellious nature of techno, seeing it as a powerful medium to express his individuality and challenge societal norms. Inspired by the pioneers of the genre, Anarchy set out on a path of sonic exploration, blending gritty industrial sounds with pulsating beats to create his signature sound.

Anarchy's performances are an assault on the senses, pushing the boundaries of what is considered acceptable in the electronic music world. His DJ sets are characterized by their relentless energy, driving rhythms, and unexpected sonic twists. With an uncanny ability to read the crowd, he creates an immersive experience that leaves audiences simultaneously exhilarated and disoriented. Anarchy's presence behind the decks is captivating, as he defies expectations and takes listeners on a journey into the depths of chaos and liberation.

In addition to his DJing prowess, Anarchy is a prolific producer, crafting tracks that are equal parts rebellious and introspective. His music is a reflection of his disdain for conformity, with distorted synths, aggressive percussion, and unconventional song structures. Anarchy's sound is a rebellion against the polished and commercialized, embracing the rough edges and imperfections that make his music stand out.

Beyond his music, Anarchy is a true advocate for the underground scene. He believes in the power of community and strives to create spaces where like-minded individuals can come together and celebrate their shared love for techno. His events are known for their immersive atmospheres, where self-expression and individuality are celebrated and encouraged.

While some may see Anarchy as a disruptor or troublemaker, he views himself as a catalyst for change. His mission is to challenge the status quo, to provoke thought, and to inspire others to embrace their inner rebels. Through his music, performances, and activism, he seeks to dismantle the barriers that stifle creativity and encourage a culture of authenticity and freedom.

Jack Anarchy is not just an artist; he is a symbol of resistance and a reminder that techno is more than just music—it's a rebellion against conformity and a celebration of individuality. As he continues to push boundaries and inspire others to embrace their true selves, Anarchy remains a beacon of defiance in the world of techno, reminding us all to question, to challenge, and to never be afraid to embrace our inner rebels.

## Helena Hauff: The Mistress of Dark Techno

Helena Hauff has emerged as one of the most captivating figures in the realm of techno, known for her uncompromising approach and atmospheric soundscapes. Hailing from Hamburg, Germany, Hauff has carved out a distinct niche for herself, captivating audiences with her dark and hypnotic blend of music.

Hauff's journey into the world of techno began at an early age, as she developed a fascination with electronic music and its ability to transport listeners to otherworldly realms. Influenced by the raw energy of industrial music, the pulsating beats of electro, and the ethereal textures of ambient, Hauff set out to create her own sonic universe, one that defied categorization and embraced the shadows.

Her DJ sets are a testament to her impeccable taste and intuitive understanding of the dancefloor. With an extensive vinyl collection at her disposal, Hauff weaves together a tapestry of sonic narratives, seamlessly blending genres and eras to create a captivating journey through sound. Her selections are often characterized by their intensity and rawness, with pounding basslines, distorted synths, and haunting melodies that transport listeners to the darkest corners of the dancefloor.

In addition to her remarkable DJ skills, Hauff is also a gifted producer. Her original tracks and remixes showcase her unique approach to music production, combining elements of acid, techno, and electro with her signature atmospheric touch. Hauff's compositions are a reflection of her introspective nature, evoking a sense of mystery and introspection that captivates listeners and leaves a lasting impression.

Beyond her artistic endeavors, Hauff is revered for her commitment to vinyl culture and her unwavering dedication to the underground scene. She is known for her extensive vinyl collection, which spans a wide range of genres and eras, and her preference for analog equipment in her production process. Her dedication to the craft is evident in every performance and release, as she remains steadfast in her mission to push the boundaries of electronic music.

Helena Hauff's impact on the techno landscape cannot be overstated. Her enigmatic persona, captivating performances, and uncompromising musical vision have earned her a devoted following around the globe. Whether she's performing in intimate clubs or headlining major festivals, Hauff's presence behind the decks is electrifying, leaving audiences in a state of awe and transcendence.

As the Mistress of Dark Techno, Helena Hauff continues to redefine the boundaries of the genre and inspire a new generation of artists and music enthusiasts. With her fearless exploration of sound and her unwavering commitment to authenticity, she stands as a beacon of creativity and individuality in the ever-evolving world of electronic music.

## The Time Eminem Fell Out with Moby

In the early 2000s, there was a highly publicized feud between the iconic rapper Eminem and the renowned musician Moby. The clash between these two artists became a topic of intense media scrutiny and sparked heated debates within the music industry.

The feud originated from an incident at the 2002 MTV Video Music Awards (VMAs) when Moby, known for his electronic music and activism, made comments in the media criticizing Eminem's lyrics and controversial content. Moby expressed his disapproval of Eminem's use of homophobic slurs and misogynistic language, stating that he found it offensive and damaging to society.

Eminem, never one to shy away from controversy, responded to Moby's remarks with a scathing diss track titled "Without Me," released as a single from his album "The Eminem Show." In the song, Eminem mocked Moby's appearance and belittled his musical career. The track gained significant attention and further intensified the feud between the two artists.

The feud escalated when Eminem referenced Moby in another diss track, "Like Toy Soldiers," which was released in 2004. In the song, Eminem accused Moby of exploiting their disagreement for publicity and criticized him for not having the same level of success or impact in the music industry.

The clash between Eminem and Moby garnered significant media coverage, with fans and industry insiders taking sides and engaging in heated debates about artistic freedom, censorship, and the responsibility of musicians. Some defended Eminem's right to express himself through his lyrics, arguing that his provocative content was a reflection of his artistry and should be protected under the principles of free speech. Others supported Moby's stance, applauding his courage to speak out against what he perceived as harmful language and attitudes in Eminem's music.

Throughout the feud, both artists maintained their positions and occasionally engaged in public exchanges through interviews and social media. However, as time passed, the intensity of the feud gradually subsided, and the two artists moved on to focus on their respective careers.

In later years, both Eminem and Moby have expressed their willingness to put the feud behind them. They have acknowledged the impact their clash had on the music industry and recognized the value of open dialogue and understanding, even in the face of artistic differences.

The feud between Eminem and Moby serves as a reminder of the power of words and the influence of music on society. It also highlights the complex dynamics within the music industry, where artistic expression often clashes with personal values and societal expectations.

While the feud between Eminem and Moby may have left a lasting impression on their careers, it also sparked important conversations about the responsibility of artists, the boundaries of artistic freedom, and the role of music as a platform for social commentary. Ultimately, it is a reminder that even in the world of music, where creative expression is celebrated, conflicts and disagreements can arise, leaving a lasting impact on the artists involved and the industry as a whole.

In the realm of music, artists often find creative ways to express their thoughts, feelings, and even frustrations. One such instance occurred when rapper Eminem used a sample in his music to take a shot at musician Moby, highlighting a clash between their musical styles and personal differences.

The sample in question can be found in Eminem's song "Without Me," released as a single from his album "The Eminem Show" in 2002. In the track, Eminem cleverly incorporates a line from Moby's song "Porcelain," a well-known track from Moby's album "Play" released in 1999. The sampled line, "Nobody listens to techno," is repeated multiple times throughout Eminem's song, serving as a playful jab at Moby and his chosen genre of music.

The inclusion of the sample in "Without Me" was not merely coincidental but rather a deliberate move by Eminem to convey a message and ignite a sense of rivalry. By sampling Moby's words, Eminem was making a statement about the perceived popularity and relevance of techno music, while simultaneously suggesting that Moby's musical style and genre were overlooked or not widely embraced by mainstream audiences.

The sample sparked controversy and drew attention to the clash between Eminem and Moby, adding fuel to an ongoing feud between the two artists. It became a talking point among fans, critics, and music enthusiasts, generating discussions about the boundaries of artistic expression, the dynamics of the music industry, and the underlying personal tensions between the artists involved.

It is important to note that the sample and subsequent use of Moby's words should be understood within the context of Eminem's provocative and often confrontational approach to music. Eminem has a history of incorporating samples and references to various artists in his work, using them as tools to convey his messages and engage in artistic dialogue.

While the sample in "Without Me" may have been seen as a direct dig at Moby and his musical style, it is worth mentioning that the clash between the two artists extended beyond the sampled line. There were underlying personal and ideological differences that contributed to the tension and animosity between them, which were further exacerbated through public statements and diss tracks.

In the realm of music, clashes and conflicts are not uncommon. They often arise from artistic differences, diverging ideologies, or personal feuds. The clash between Eminem and Moby, encapsulated in the sampled line "Nobody listens to techno," represents a moment where these tensions surfaced and became a focal point of discussion within the music industry.

Over time, the feud between Eminem and Moby has faded, as both artists have moved on to focus on their respective careers and creative endeavors. Nevertheless, the sample in "Without Me" remains a notable part of their shared history, representing a chapter in the ever-evolving landscape of music and the complex dynamics that exist within it.

While the sampled line may have sparked controversy and fueled the clash between Eminem and Moby, it also serves as a testament to the power of music to provoke, challenge, and engage audiences in dialogue about artistic expression and the diversity of musical genres.

## Conclusion: Reflecting on the History of Techno Music

As we come to the end of this journey through the history of techno music, we are reminded of the profound impact this genre has had on the music industry and the cultural landscape. From its humble origins in Detroit to its global reach today, techno has evolved, adapted, and continued to captivate audiences around the world.

Throughout this book, we have explored the key chapters that have shaped techno's trajectory. We delved into the origins of sound, tracing its roots from Detroit to Berlin and the influential figures who pioneered its development. We witnessed the birth of techno through the Belleville Three and the emergence of the underground warehouse scene that gave it a platform to thrive.

We examined the pioneers of techno, such as Juan Atkins and Derrick May, whose innovative sounds laid the foundation for the genre's future. We explored the expansion of Detroit techno and its influence on artists like Inner City and Model 500, as well as the European takeover that spread techno across the continent.

We witnessed the revolution that accompanied the fall of the Berlin Wall and the fusion of techno with the political and social changes of the time. We explored the impact of acid house and the rise of UK rave culture, as well as the mainstream success and crossover hits that propelled techno into new realms.

We ventured into the world of techno subgenres, from ambient and industrial to hardcore, and explored how these variations contributed to the genre's diversity and evolution. We witnessed techno's global influence, as it transcended borders and found its place in electronic music scenes worldwide.

We examined the transformative power of techno in the digital age, with the rise of DJs and producers who reshaped the landscape of the genre. We witnessed techno's role as a form of resistance, providing a voice for political and social movements that sought change and liberation.

We explored the vibrant culture of techno festivals and the communal experience of raving, where music and movement merge to create an immersive and transcendent atmosphere. We looked ahead to the future, contemplating the continued evolution of techno music and the visions that will shape its path.

Throughout this journey, we have encountered the stories of countless artists, innovators, and visionaries who have contributed to the tapestry of techno music. Their dedication, creativity, and passion have propelled the genre forward, pushing boundaries and challenging conventions.

Techno music, with its pulsating rhythms, hypnotic beats, and futuristic sounds, continues to resonate with audiences across generations. Its influence can be felt in various genres and its impact on the music industry is undeniable.

As we conclude this book, we invite you to immerse yourself in the world of techno music. Explore its rich history, discover its diverse subgenres, and embrace the unique energy that it brings. Whether you find yourself on a dancefloor, in a club, or listening to the beats in the comfort of your own space, let techno transport you to a realm where the past, present, and future converge.

The history of techno music is an ever-evolving narrative, and we can only speculate about the exciting chapters that lie ahead. As new artists emerge, technologies advance, and societal shifts occur, techno music will continue to evolve, adapt, and inspire.

So, let the rhythms of the future guide your journey, as the history of techno music lives on, forever shaping the soundscapes of our world.

Thank you for joining us on this exploration of the history of techno music. May the beats continue to resonate within you, and may the spirit of techno guide you on your own musical odyssey.

**Ladies and gentlemen,**

Today, I stand before you to share my deep passion and love for techno music, a genre that has become the very essence of my artistic expression. As many of you may know, I am David Jack Gregg, and I want to take this opportunity to shed light on my journey as a techno producer, working under the alias of Jack Anarchy.

Techno music has always held a special place in my heart. Its driving beats, hypnotic rhythms, and intricate soundscapes have the power to transport listeners to another dimension, where time and space intertwine. From the very first moment I experienced the pulsating energy on a dimly lit dancefloor, I knew I had discovered a world that would forever shape my creative path.

Under the guise of Jack Anarchy, I have embarked on a sonic exploration, delving into the depths of techno's vast sonic palette. It is a journey of self-discovery, a constant quest to push boundaries, challenge conventions, and create music that resonates with the souls of those who listen.

Techno, for me, is not simply a genre of music; it is a way of life. It embodies the essence of rebellion, freedom, and raw emotion. It speaks to the core of our existence, transcending language and cultural barriers. Through my productions, I aim to capture the essence of these emotions, to create sonic landscapes that evoke a visceral response within the listener.

In the studio, I lose myself in a realm of synthesizers, drum machines, and samplers, meticulously crafting each element to build a sonic journey that takes the listener on an immersive experience. It is in these moments of creation that I feel truly alive, where time ceases to exist, and I am consumed by the sheer euphoria of the music I am creating.

But my love for techno goes beyond the confines of the studio. It extends to the dancefloor, where I have had the privilege of witnessing the transformative power of music. There is something truly magical about the energy shared between DJ and crowd, as the beats resonate through every fiber of our being, creating an interconnectedness that unites us all.

Techno, at its core, is about connection. It transcends individuality and creates a sense of unity among those who embrace its sonic embrace. It is this communal spirit that continues to inspire me, driving me to create music that ignites a fire within, music that brings people together and evokes a sense of shared experience.

Through the medium of Jack Anarchy, I aim to contribute to the ever-evolving tapestry of techno music. I aspire to create tracks that leave an indelible mark on the hearts and minds of those who listen, tracks that carry the energy of the dancefloor and the passion that fuels my artistic soul.

Techno has the power to shape our world, to challenge norms, and to ignite change. It is a force that demands to be heard and felt. I am humbled and honored to be a part of this movement, and I am eternally grateful to all those who have supported and believed in me on this musical journey.

In closing, I would like to express my heartfelt gratitude to all the fellow techno enthusiasts, the dancers, the DJs, the producers, and the entire techno community. Your unwavering passion and dedication inspire me daily and push me to evolve as an artist.

Together, let us continue to embrace the power of techno, to create, to dance, and to forge a future where the beats of our collective heartbeat to the rhythm of our shared dreams.

Thank you for taking the time to read this book, "Rhythms of the Future: The History of Techno Music." It has been a pleasure to guide you through the fascinating journey of techno's origins, its evolution, and its enduring impact on the global music scene.

Techno music is more than just a genre; it is a cultural phenomenon that has transcended borders and captured the hearts and minds of people around the world. From its humble beginnings in Detroit to its international expansion, techno has become a powerful force that continues to shape the way we experience and appreciate music.

Throughout the chapters, we have explored the pioneers who laid the foundation for techno, such as the Belleville Three and the Techno Pioneers like Juan Atkins and Derrick May. We have witnessed how the underground movement and warehouse scenes birthed a new wave of musical expression and brought techno to the forefront of nightlife culture.

The book also delved into the impact of techno's subgenres, such as ambient, industrial, and hardcore, showcasing the versatility and diversity within the genre. We examined how techno crossed continents, influencing electronic music worldwide and leaving an indelible mark on different cultures and scenes.

As we delved into the digital age, we witnessed the rise of DJs and producers, who utilized technology to push the boundaries of sound and create immersive experiences for their audiences. We explored the role of techno as a form of resistance, driving political and social movements, and examined the culture of raving and the significance of techno festivals.

The final chapters provided insights into the current techno scene, highlighting the thriving scenes in cities like London, Brighton, and beyond. We discussed the popularity of techno today compared to its early days in the '90s and explored the profiles of top techno DJs, including Nina Kraviz, Adam

Beyer, Amelie Lens, Charlotte de Witte, Ben Klock, Jack Anarchy, Helena Hauff, and others.

Through the pages of this book, I hope you have gained a deeper appreciation for the rich history, cultural significance, and artistic brilliance of techno music. It is a testament to the power of creativity, innovation, and the unwavering passion of the artists and enthusiasts who continue to drive the genre forward.

Thank you once again for embarking on this journey through the history of techno music. May the beats of techno continue to inspire, unite, and shape the rhythms of our future.

David Jack Gregg.

Printed in Great Britain
by Amazon

24194849R00033